MOVEMENTS IN MODERN ART

CUBISM

MOVEMENTS IN MODERN ART

ALFRED SCHMELLER

CUBISM

WITH 24 ILLUSTRATIONS

15032

CROWN PUBLISHERS, INC.

NEW YORK

Translated by Hilde Spiel

Reproduction Rights: S.P.A.D.E.M., Paris, and Cosmopress, Geneva
Printed in Austria
by Brüder Rosenbaum, Vienna

CUBISM

One day, long after the birth of Cubism, Picasso and the art dealer Daniel Henry Kahnweiler were searching their memories for the year in which it took place. They remembered that between April and May 1907 Picasso had begun to paint a canvas, about 8 foot square, which was subsequently known as "Les Demoiselles d'Avignon" and which now hangs in the Museum of Modern Art in New York. This picture may indeed be considered to have been the point of departure of a new phase in painting, called Cubism.

The origin of the term is uncertain. It is said that Henri Matisse, the initiator of another artistic movement, Fauvism, while a member of the jury at the Paris Salon of 1908, remarked in front of Georges Braque's paintings: "Trop de cubes!" (Too many cubes). On the other hand it was the art critic L. Vauxcelles who, in his review of a Braque exhibition at Kahnweiler's, talked of "petits cubes" and later of "bizarreries cubes". This was but a superficial description of the pictures, for it was not the painter's intention to transform reality, as it were by a stroke of the brush, into so many erratic blocks. But as so often happens in the history of art, a half-mocking, half-critical remark was taken up, used as a label and henceforth attached to a new direction in style. Soon the painters Picasso, Braque, Fernand Léger and a little later Juan Gris, issuing from many different parts of the world and various schools of art, joined forces in Paris and, recognizing their common aim, professed themselves members of the "Cubist family". Guillaume Apollinaire, the poet and spokesman of the group, in his preface to the first foreign Cubist exhibition at Brussels in 1911, finally put the official seal on this expression.

The landscape of Estaque painted by Braque on the shores of the Mediterranean in 1908, which is reproduced on plate 1 of this volume, gives some idea of the manner of Braque and Picasso in the years of the "Demoiselles d'Avignon". These pictures broke away violently from the artistic conception of the Fauves, the "wild beasts" who, since 1905, had been considered the *dernier cri* in the art of the metropolis.

Every artistic movement of our time has begun by renouncing its predecessor. Naturally the artists had studied the work of their somewhat older colleagues with a careful and critical eye. The platform reached by their predecessors served them as a jumping-board. For several years Braque had fallen in with the Fauves and, at the age of 22, finished his apprenticeship with them. Although at the turn of the century artists and groups of artists worked in far greater isolation from one another than they do today, and were by no means always known to each other or inclined to form a "clique" — Kahnweiler, the art dealer of the Cubists, at that time knew neither Vuillard nor Bonnard, nor Lautrec, and of that generation only Redon — yet communication established itself between them in some mysterious way. Picasso had already passed through several periods: an Impressionist, a lyrical, a Lautrec-period, and a period of *Weltschmerz*. By determining his own position, every artist fixed his fellows in their respective places. To Matisse, the Impressionist paintings appeared a veritable mass of contradictions; yet thirty years earlier their creators, unable to conform with the static, heroic and romantic pose of their contemporaries, had been cast in the role of rabid revolutionaries, and even now the storm aroused by their pictures had not yet died down. Courbet, Manet, Monet, Cézanne, Matisse, and Picasso — every one of these painters caused a revolution, took his stand against existing formulae, and pressed on, until all doors leading to our century were thrown open. Retrospectively, the logical way in which they unfolded in all directions becomes clear; it resembles a rocket breaking up in the air and scattering its components from which, in turn, new clusters of stars shoot up, explode, and so on ad infinitum.

Even so it remains strange that all of a sudden Picasso should treat his pictures with such brutality, hack about his faces until they begin to leer, and ram black outlines into his paintings as though with his bare fists. He seems to have been gripped by a tremendous outburst of fury. Yet there is little or no connection between this outburst and the theoretical aims which two years later he was to pursue and which Apollinaire was in due course to define. In 1908 Braque, too, achieved this power of expression which makes the deformation introduced by the Fauves look like a comparatively harmless conceit. The razor-like sharpness of Picasso's faces and limbs first appears in his drawings of 1905 and 1906, in the metal-edge outlines of eyebrows and noses in his female heads, and in the cold delineation of his circus folk. In the same year Léger begins to express, in a hard and sober way, his

6

Plate 4

Georges Braque (born 1882 at Argenteuil)

THE PORTUGUESE

Oil, painted 1911

Kunstmuseum, Basle

A painting full of noise. It is a cataract of single sounds, a convulsive shifting of outbursts, knocks and shouts. The hard angular atmosphere evokes associations: a port, dockers, steam ships, a clatter of timber, a creaking of pulleys, the noise of loading. Letters are stencilled as on bales or boxes. The punched-out angular shapes recall jerky movements. Shapes formed like roofs are built up high, in between steam goes up. The composition resembles a spire. Instead of objects there are merely abridgements. Everything here twitches, chops, vibrates. The painting consists of nothing but interruptions. Its colours are those of evening mist and ship's timber.

Plate 5

Georges Braque (born 1882 at Argenteuil)

ACE OF CLUBS

Oil, painted around 1911

Musée National d'Art Moderne, Paris

There is no need to feel confused by the apparent disorderliness of this painting. A somewhat strenuous visual exercise is needed to read it, but lazy eyes are taxed no less by a Viking ornament, an Oriental carpet or Rembrandt's "Night Watch". The picture is determined mainly by vertical lines; horizontal lines are in the minority, and oblique ones still more infrequent. The vertical lines are fluted channels, that is, edges collecting shadows. Dominant among the curved lines is the circular form somewhat below the centre, a black table top seen from above, in the centre of which rests an ace of hearts. However, the picture as a whole is seen neither entirely from above, nor from the front; nor are these two views blended. It is divided up into areas which are frequently varied, superimposed on each other and joggled, and which correspond to, or contrast with, each other across short distances, expressing either a material object or its structure. The painting comes nearest to a *bas relief*. The black circle is stuck with trapezoid shapes grained like wood — like a winged wheel — and held together, in the bottom centre, by a fragment of panelling. The ingenious manner in which forms are integrated in multifarious ways, suggesting a number of objects arranged as a still-life, seems to lend wings to this painting.

Plate 6

Georges Braque (born 1882 at Argenteuil)

GLASS AND NEWSPAPER

Oil, painted 1912

Collection Gustav Zumsteg, Zurich

A picture in the old sense of the term came into being as though in a looking-glass. The calmly contemplating eye of the painter was the silverfoil taking in the whole of reality and transferring it bit by bit, with the help of a brush, onto the canvas. Reality thus seems to pre-exist in its entirety, and the picture frame cuts out a piece from it. You may penetrate such a picture, proceding from the larger context to the smaller, from the room to the chair, on to the leg of the chair, and to the light reflected on polished wood. There is a common relationship full of calm, static, illusory in space, complete at every point, material, and governed by a central perspective. One object covers another or bars it from view. The contemplating eye proceeds by method of deduction.

Cubist pictures are created differently. Partial impressions rush together, overlapping and overlaying each other all the time. It is not the subject as such which is transfixed on the canvas, but a momentary impression or, to the same effect, a scrap of memory which is noted down. This type of painting is adapted to the psychological condition of modern man. The speed with which stimuli assail us from the outside or inside, to vanish again, to flit by, or to leave a small puncture in our perception, results in their fragmentary assimilation, their accumulation in layers and their mutual influence on each other. In Braque's painting the vibrating cinematographic effect is quite pronounced. In their swift progress optic stimuli cut each other short, become transparent or penetrate each other. Nothing is at rest but the painter who splits things up into their fragments and shapes them into a picture — just as the Futurist divides up the movement of things into its moments. Reality is not destroyed but merely perceived in an up-to-date manner In this the Cubists, unlike the Impressionists, do not aim at an illusion of wholeness, but compose their pictures from particles, from a continually shifting point of view. The contemplating eye achieves a synthesis. These pictures are symptomatic of the quick pace of our century.

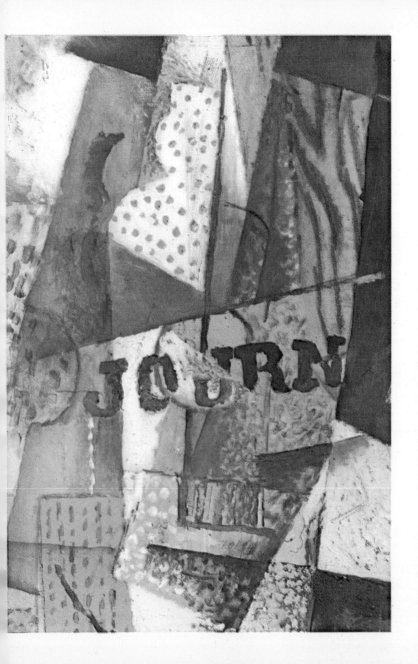

Plate 7

Pablo Picasso (born 1881 at Malaga)

THE VIOLIN

Oil, painted 1914

Musée National d'Art Moderne, Paris

After a while, the attempt to correlate objects in a context is abandoned. Here are fields of colour, painted but plainly derived from the *papier collé* — among them patterned paper which might be used to line a violin-case — or simply colour sounds, clear, velvety, dull, and around the edges chirping ones. One shape overlays the other, covering the preceding one, although the outline is traced through. Some of the sheets stand out from those underneath, as for instance the playing-card, but this too is traversed by a shaded edge. Thus air is allowed to penetrate between the layers which have fluttered down like the torn-off leaves of a calendar. The silt of time has accumulated, layer upon layer, in the shape of waste paper (*jour*, the day, is visible as part of the word *journal*). The succession of area chords forms a kind of scaffolding decorated around the edges with symbolic abbreviations — a violin-peg, the ace of clubs, the journal, a flute (?), the fret-board of a guitar. The word BASS and above it the abbreviation of a bottle recur in other still-lifes of that year. The central area seems to move in slow clockwise rotation. The picture resembles the face of a grandfather clock, but there are ciphers instead of figures. It is the musical score of a still-life. From time to time something rattles, and the pendulum swings to and fro. "Jour" stands for the days sinking away, one after the other. The "works" have been dismantled, yet go on functioning; they collect spatial and material objects while time ticks on, they scatter symbols of objects on the dial. Picasso gives his picture the spell-binding power of old-fashioned automatic toys; it moves like the mechanism of a rifle-range at the fair, set in motion by a bulls-eye.

Plate 8

Fernand Léger (born 1881 at Argentan, died 1955)

WOMAN IN GREEN AND RED

Oil, painted 1914

Musée National d'Art Moderne, Paris

The painting and wheezing of technical life have rushed into the very forms of this picture, like the devil into the Gadarene swine. Everything pushes, knocks, whistles, steams, hisses and rumbles, everything is made up of pipes, funnels, engine parts, steel axles, piston-rods and protective cover to keep out the hot breath of the engine. During a certain period the turbulent world of factory life seemed to rattle through the art of Léger, a world of steaming impressions. Later all this was clarified, rendered static and stabilized. Nowadays there are even industrial designers. Labour, energy, productive strength are here "realized", as well as those feats of strength which even woman must perform — every kitchen being a small chemical factory, every cooking stove constituting a heating plant in little, every dwelling containing a number of machines. To realize, make real (*réaliser*) was a favourite expression of Cézanne's. Thus the picture is transformed: it is no longer woman who is here depicted, but a spiritual impetus, that of work, which is "realized" and made palpable and visible. In fact, the picture is no longer a picture. It is a solid object, in itself materialized energy.

Plate 9

Juan Gris (born 1887 in Madrid, died 1927)

STILL-LIFE

Oil, painted 1917

Musée National d'Art Moderne, Paris

Jug and chair. Matter has turned into a blast of energy, and from it the jug shoots down onto the chair. A conical headlight picks out its shape. One object is caught in the energy radius of another. The ribs of the back of the chair are repeated and contrasted in the arched shadow of the jug. The chair fans out. The jug, on the other hand, is concentrated and tapers off into a cone, again to contrast with the chair. It is arranged in accordance with the lower outline of the chair and rests on it like a pyramid. The container sits there as on a throne, surrounded by an aureole. The chair-legs and their edges strictly speaking no longer "belong" to the chair, but are related, within the movement of composition, to the adjacent space, from which they jut out. Nothing here is smoothly joined, forms are related by way of a harsh command, a severe control, by a lightning check. This is an interrogation by searchlight. The jug has a wicked stare. Jug and chair are visibly integrated between searchlight and aureole.

Plate 10

Jean Metzinger (born 1883 in Nantes)

KNITTING WOMAN

Oil, painted 1919

Musée National d'Art Moderne, Paris

A busy picture. The Cubist method is well demonstrated, even somewhat too distinctly, so that the part played by the unconscious is neglected. As an instructional pattern this picture is easy to "read". It is completely saturated with the activity of knitting. The needles, describing sectors of a circle, carry out swift movements which extend over the whole figure. At the same time, table, carpet, and wall are at rest — level formations which serve as a calm, quiet foil. The centre part of the picture is as jerkily agitated as are the knitting needles. Where the needles meet lies the pivotal point. From it vibrations radiate in all directions, terminating in areas which block their advance. Three such main centres can be found in a vertical line — at the knees, between the hands, and at the chin. From these points the circular movements emanate to meet each other.

In order to portray the three-dimensional activity of knitting within the two-dimensional area of the picture, spherical sections are treated like two-dimensional areas intertwining, overlayed on, or slipped into, each other.

The deflections of the knitting needles suggest the limits set to our vision of any given object. The ends are correlated, each end echoing the one opposite. The main transversal sections are

1. the white area traversed by

2. a blue area composed of the left shoulder, the lower part of the skirt, the right sleeve and the left half of the face,

3. the dark area rising from the shadow of the chair (waves — the joints — are swelling up from the chair-legs).

These areas constitute in every case the framework of a similar form — inset form — in front of them. The piece of knitting lies within the white area of light and is divided up into a spotted and a shaded half. The spotted upholstery of the chair lies within the shadow zone, the ball of wool within the paper, the paper within the table top, the left hand within a brown card which seems to have been slotted into the picture. There are thus several pictures within the picture. The jug on the table is no jug but the picture of a jug, a jug mirrored and reflected. When the picture is knitted together in our vision, more correlations will emerge. Temporal movements are transformed into areas which cut obliquely through space. The interweaving of space and time becomes apparent, perhaps a little too obviously so; the involuntary part of creation is missing. While knitting, the woman counts the stitches. She is a Penelope gathering up seconds in time.

Plate 11

Georges Braque (born 1882)

STILL-LIFE WITH FRUIT BOWL

Oil, painted 1919

Musée National d'Art Moderne, Paris

Again the composite shape is there before it is split up into its components. A bowl of fruit in brittle outline, seen as a section, clutching its contents like an open hand. Although seemingly dipped in moonlight and subdued in colour, some individual parts assert their independence. A colour smudge marks the place where something was drowned, leaving a remnant. A still-life like a landscape.

Much is gained by comparing this picture to the still-life with a similar subject by Juan Gris (Plate 12). Gris' still-life is cool and spreads out bit by bit, like an umbrella unfolding. In Braque's painting everything is dominated by an area like a planed beach, like the shallows — metamorphic, dreamy, mellow, balanced, mature age-old, and full of suggestions of an ancient civilization.

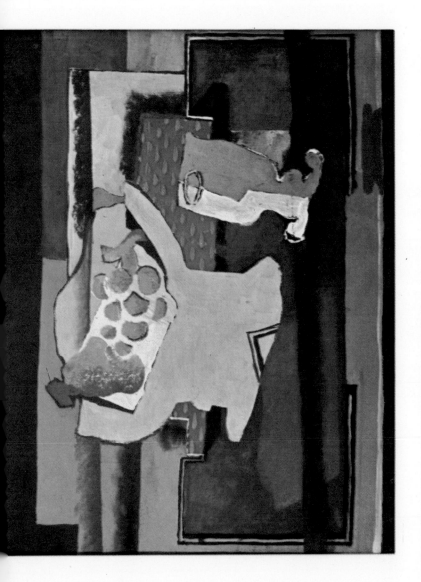

Plate 12

Juan Gris (born 1887 in Madrid, died 1927 in Paris)

STILL-LIFE

Oil, painted 1921

Kunstmuseum, Basle, Emanuel Hoffmann Donation

Having picked out, from the context of this composition, the figures of the vase, the bowl of fruit, and the grapes, one is tempted to assume that a steamroller must have gone over the picture and flattened it. Indeed all objects seem compressed into each other. It is the secret of this picture, however, that it is not flat, but that the colour areas stand out against each other, are placed at an angle, are projecting outward although they are fused into unity. Areas forming the background and areas jutting out in space are counter-balanced; as soon as this is recognized, the picture magically stirs to life. Now the walls, the tablecloth, the decanter, the bowl and the fruit disengage themselves from the dark background and build up a separate space before us which the eye can penetrate from various angles. The objects are not placed into a given space, but space itself unfolds angularly, thrustingly, in unison with the objects.

Plate 13

Pablo Picasso (born 1881)

STILL-LIFE

Oil, painted 1922

Musée National d'Art Moderne, Paris

Another still-life. The presumption and banality of the world of objects has been re-composed. Objects have been reduced to ciphers. Table, guitar, bowl, and vase are pricked out in angular outlines. Shaded areas are ribbed. The whole has been attuned to the signal colours of the *tricolor*. This concentration upon sign language, outlined gestures, cross hatching and signal call, required colour and line to be separated like pulp from juice. Colour and line anyway are suppositions which do not occur in nature, mere abstractions, as can be seen whenever a still-life is held against nature.

Plate 14

Joan Mirò (born 1893 at Montroig, Barcelona)

THE FARMER'S WIFE

Painted 1922/23

Collection Mme Alexina S. Duchamp, New York

This picture is completely filled with yellow, the dry straw-coloured yellow of a day when the threshing-machine has been running from morning till night.

It is included in this series because it indicates how Cubism affected painters following entirely different paths. Although it bears many features of the Cubist method, mixed here with a naive realism — the cat might have been painted by the Douanier Rousseau — it is no purely Cubist picture.

There is no need to describe the painting, as the agricultural scene is most faithfully reproduced. What is Cubist in it is the shifting in space brought about by a partition of areas; by the contrasting of axles (for instance the cat and the plate) and of level details with roundly plastic ones (feet against toes); and by the "false" plasticity (hamper, hare's belly, cheeks of farmer's wife, hem of her dress). Cubism might also claim for itself the grotesque intensity which emphasises the meaning. The feet which are larger-than-life, the rigid hare's fur, the working hands. Human features are objectified and equated to objects; perhaps because of the archaic character of a farmer's working world, which completely justifies this primitive treatment.

weariness with the exuberance of the Fauves. All of a sudden there evolve within the confines of a canvas energies such as had not emerged in European art for centuries as openly, as unrepressed. Even then it was possible to divine something of the dynamics about to be let loose in politics, in the social upheaval, in the mass movements and technical development of our century.

This violence has often been traced to the influence of Negro sculpture which at that time began to fascinate some of the painters. In fact, what happened was rather the reverse — the onrush of the catastrophic opened everyone's eyes to the elementary power of primitive art. African sculpture is wholly dominated by symmetry, while in Cubist art features, limbs, and strips of land slide into each other with angular vehemence, knock each other like piston-rods, or tumble down pell-mell, bursting into fragments, as though hit by lightning. Cubist, prismatic and pyramidal forms are not heavily and weightily at rest like the stones of an edifice, but are set in motion — pictures of an earthquake.

Gradually, the conception is clarified. Forms are polished like crystal and brought out with ever sharper edges. And so, at last, the new tendency emerges; it aims at a decomposition of the plastic image. For that reason the first Cubist period has been called the *analytical*. It lasted from 1909 till 1912, and its initial phase was very aptly defined as "Facet Cubism". If the term "analytical" is used in the current sense, by which different aspects of one and the same object, its front, back and side views, are fused and integrated within one picture, it can be applied here only in a limited way. If, however, "analysis" is understood to mean the close scrutiny of the corporeal qualities of an object — of its density and action, of the way it juts out and recedes, caves in, protrudes, and thrusts forward — and the representation of these bodily activities by means of broken surfaces and prismatically creased wedges — facets — interlocked like so many hinges, then the paintings of 1909/10 are much more exactly described.

It is tempting to assume that the variety of aspects introduced by Facet Cubism was achieved in front of the original subject, and that these artists compressed and joined together different views of nature on one canvas. But Picasso and Braque had already cut loose from the set pattern, the prototype of nature, and had begun to paint from memory. This constitutes a turning-point in art.

The Impressionists had gone out to nature and into the open air; all their purpose had been directed towards the representation of reality. Cézanne, too, had constantly corrected his own perception of form by looking at nature, at landscape, at motifs such as groups of trees, valleys, and the outlines of mountains. The Cubists returned to the studio and worked from memory. Their view was thus freed from the limitations of reality. It was no longer their aim to create spatial illusions related to reality, but to create irrational space, their own invented space, a transcendental world which differed altogether from the everyday world of our experience. Painting became poetry again. They dispensed with real colours, with blue for the sky — as Monet had re-discovered it — with green for grass and brown for tree-trunks. The Cubists bid one enter rooms of glass, cooler grottoes where the bluegreen of the sea-bed predominates, a whole world of hallucination where "light seems reluctantly to pour out into a void". This endeavour has nothing to do with chaos and the dissolution of reality, as wide-spread slogans reviling the "disruptive and Nihilist tendencies of modern art" have tried to make out. When, for instance, one of the Impressionists, Renoir, painted "Peaches, Figs and Almonds", the result was a figment of spots and patches, an image of air and fragrance and specks of light, which maintained its colourful independence from palpable reality. This withdrawal from a compact world which was tangible, palpable and therefore also destructible, was the decisive step. It was the basis for all further experiments. These, however, would aim, not at the demolition of reality, but at the building-up of new images which shared with reality only their proneness to destruction. It is a most common error to judge modern art from a pre-Impressionist point-of-view, and to examine just how faithful is its image of nature. The Cubists merely used certain relics of objects, figures and landscape, in order to discover new kinds of form and space; they remembered the world as one remembers the fantastic past of the fairy tales, the diamond mountain or bizarre rocky scenery which Sinbad the Sailor passed in his travels. In this respect Facet Cubism is a miraculous art and fundamentally opposed to Cézanne's obstinate adherence to his subject, though the perception of space remained the basis of his art.

Even the first Cubist landscapes of Picasso, Braque and Léger (plates 1 and 2) are tight and compact, admitting no view out into open atmosphere;

they are shut in as though blocked by scenery, and their space appears semi-liquid and impenetrable. Instead of air, they seem filled with an opaque mass. Thus even an open landscape is made to look like an interior, and space is turned inside out. We see no free spatial extension, but a hollow world shut in on all sides. Blinking facets give the impression of crystal enclosures in barren rock. In Cézanne's paintings space no longer lent itself to penetration by the illusioned eye, it had become inaccessible despite the fact that his landscapes and interiors had been obtained from direct observation. The peep-show quality of pictures had been reduced by the Impressionists; Cézanne had equally balanced surface and space in his paintings; but analytical Cubism made them impenetrable. All that was left were niches in the irrational, a refuge here and there in a tumbling world, the hollow hands of a remote deity. Cézanne's artistic equation brought in its wake a disarrangement and blocking-up of reality; but Cubism signified a turning away from imitation and a suspension of the laws of proportion which had lost all meaning in a world no longer arithmetically controlled. The elongated arm of Cézanne's "Boy with the red Waistcoat" became, in the art of Braque, a motorial gesture, a subterfuge, a creaking transmission gear; ("The Portuguese", plate 4.) In that early phase of fermentation Cézanne was re-cast, cooled down to a glassy still-life, and finally broken up into convulsively vibrating particles of matter.

It was not until the advent of Cubism that painting shook free from the grip of everyday life. Now the gulf became so wide that it seemed impossible to see a picture as a whole. The impenetrable space of the first Cubist canvases appears to be stamped into the parchment of old book bindings. Many paintings by Juan Gris give one a feeling of reading a book without turning its pages. But for the material existence of the blots of paint, one might believe them to be notes concerning objects painted on a sheet of glass. But the fine verve of these light browns, these few blues and greys is anything but smooth, so that it is impossible to look through the pastily covered canvas as one might look through plate glass. Space as seen through a peephole, space as of a box, space conceived as a relief are abandoned. Illusion now is not only impenetrable, but also completely opaque, yet at the same time of utter clarity. By common agreement this phase is called "Hermetical Cubism". It ran its course during 1910 and 1911.

The painter's attitude has gained in distinction. Memory is now sovereign. There is a return to the world of objects, to the stage where palpable drama takes place. At the same time, the gradual extinction of the object is being accomplished. What remain are hooked shapes; angular recesses wherein is found a residue of tender blue; the neck of a violin alternating with a treble clef, or emerging within a spiral scroll; crotchets and quavers; the edge of a table; or letters — it is a disparate and nervous vision, flatly engraved. Objects do not yield at once. Febrile, trembling and vibrating, they are being softly drummed together by means of the tiniest glass prisms. They are no more than a hint, the beating of a wing against the membrane of the conscious, a fleeting touch. They are a game played with beads of glass. Others suggest a slightly rattling glass door opening into a small bar-room. Sounds drip down a window-pane. Frequently during that period, it is almost impossible to tell Picasso's paintings from Braque's, although Braque is a shade warmer, still a shade more nervous. These pictures hum, they are symphonic pictures whose details make up a harmony of sounds suggesting objects. This phase might suitably be called the "musical", also taking into account the fact that on its canvases musical instruments such as the violin and the guitar are often represented.

An assonance of excited particles in the shape of colour sounds or blots of paint may meet the request for an object, a violin or a portrait head, to be captured in its completeness. This aim at totality demands not only that the passage of time should be fixed in space, but also that causality and the classic conception of unity of time and space should be abandoned. For this reason the object is divided up into partial impressions which the eye, rather painfully at first, must piece together. One after another it registers: an ace of clubs, arched shapes, grapes, grained wood (ah, a table!), the rim of a bowl, shadows, letters (probably from the mast-head of a newspaper). This "after one another", however, is united in the humming "together", in the assonance. The viewer's eye is continuously stimulated and made to follow along an incessant string of associations which have risen up from the painter's well of memories and left their traces on the canvas. He knows: over the white canvas have whisked a violin, or a vase, or a pack of cards, whose imprints, on a plane accessible to the viewer, are now inter-locked as though in a tooth-gearing. The footprints of reality are mixed up by memory like a hand of cards held by someone ignorant of the rules of the game.

Painters paint what they know, what flows together in their consciousness; they associate, they form a community of remembered remnants of reality, of elements far removed from each other in space and time. A new dimension is thus introduced; it is remembrance, the inner region which sends off, bit by bit, and in ever new variety, messages which are the marks of time, the notches, incisions and scars in the conscious mind. But how banal, on their return, these memories often seem! So much, if no more, should be said in defence of Cubist painters.

This region of the soul, clinging to objects and materializing in objects, is translated into two-dimensional language. We all know about transmission in a bicycle and the changing of gears in a motor car. The relation between a painter's conception of reality and the finished picture is a comparable process, except that the picture is not a mechanism, and the structure of the object, in being hauled up from the conscious, is broken up, stretched and liquified. Mechanically-minded people, therefore, are wont to point out in front of these pictures that they simply wouldn't function.

In a portrait of Picasso Juan Gris tried to rationalize the method — there is no flaw in its construction. This is a play on the figure three; there are three colours, three ways for the light to enter and the shadow to fall. In a way, three dimensions are projected onto the same area, and these three - directional impulses are interlocked like the parts of an engine. The principal colour is grey, supported by shades of beige, blue and purple which form metallic reflections. With Gris these reflections are important; he values the mirror-effect. In contrast to the muted tones of Picasso and Braque, his paintings are vividly coloured. Another of his characteristics is a peculiarly frayed tension of line and colour. His lines curve apart, they spread asunder like the wires of a flex, yet retain their elasticity. Colour is treated in a similar way; he puts crimson against blue and straw-colour, dusty wallpaper-pink against a deep sky-blue. Behind a wash-stand he inserts the real fragments of a looking-glass which flash into the viewer's eyes. Not merely is the world split up on his canvas, but contemplation itself is being split through a momentary blinding which affects the eye.

The phase which follows is marked by the introduction of true remnants of reality into the picture: pieces of a mirror, genuine bits of wallpaper, newspaper cuttings etc. It was said by Alfred Barr, (to whom — next to Carl Einstein and Klaus Demus — we owe much insight into the nature of Cubism as well as its classification in phases,) that here we see broken up, for the first time since medieval Gothic, the unity of the artist's medium: paint applied by a brush. Yet with the technique of *collage*, the stick-on picture, Cubism enters a phase of calm and clarification. Here, primarily, single areas are set off against each other, although within itself each is formally homogeneous. Colour tensions are increased, contrasts are more pronounced. The assonance is sounded in single notes which are maintained for a longer period. Somewhere in the painting there is a pause. Impulses are less violently directed against each other, and all run parallel to the picture. This is no longer a symphony, but chamber music. Juan Gris' trio has been mentioned. These pictures have less in common with a daydream, they are less trance-like, more sober, more material, more of this world, but at the same time more abysmal, fetishistic, spell-binding and, if possible, even more daring in their spiritual tension. They lead to the phase of "Synthetic Cubism."

With Picasso, this phase lasted roughly from 1913 until well into the twenties, with Gris until his death in 1927. Braque was to develop, within its orbit, his own, cosier style which may be said to have lasted, with certain interruptions and other influences, up to the present. From now on the roads of the great masters of Cubism diverge, although occasionally they meet again or evoke each other. Picasso in particular, eternally re-born, passes through so many stages that, to put it at its most extreme, nearly every new painting of his constitutes a new phase. His work is itself a time-space continuum. From 1918 onwards Cubism influenced an ever-growing number of painters so that no art may be said to exist "which was not anointed with a drop of Cubist oil" (Kahnweiler). But it is impossible to deal with all developments which followed without going beyond the limits of this introduction.

Synthetic Cubism, to put it crudely, is dominated by the re-appearance of the object, be it in the context of a still-life, be it in a composition of figures. Yet the emergence of the *thing* does not signify a return to the timid portrayal of reality. There is always an ample drop of Cubist oil in the paint. However, whereas up to 1913 all elements of a picture had to be added up, now the object is no longer split in fragments but summarized. Now indeed its totality can be seized at one go. Always, of course, the relation of the object to the structure of the painting must be explored, but this relation has become more complex. Now all impulses are directed towards the object, instead of perpetually leading upwards and sideways. The object is associated with its context as though they were intertwined. For that reason the dominant characteristic of this phase has been found to be the inter-relation of shape. Its product is not the time-space continuum, but the continuum of the object whose qualities are nevertheless marked out by space and time.

The object is made to submit to certain primary descriptions of form. When it is measured off geometrically, the angular areas are sharply contrasted in pure and unbroken colours. When it is embedded in soft contours, it is also immersed in softly shaded hues. Painful isolation corresponds to a sharp metallic edge. Marble streaks seem to drip viscously or to crumble with brittle colour. Although this has been varied in dozens of still-lifes, it is no mere artistic game.

The character of one of these pictures is closely akin to form and colour — colour being understood as a quality of form. As a result of this the object once more acquires greater significance; it is formally functionalized. Form, here, is a function of character-shape. Around 1911 the object was near extinction. With the object re-acquired, it can now be measured, but its proportions are of a different order. The object is now capable of extension, stretching and transformation according to its capacity for action.

One may well wonder why Picasso, in the early twenties, suddenly passed through a classic phase. But the so-called "Ingres Period" was no arbitrary step. Picasso's relapse was no charlatanry, but a way of proving his point. At closer inspection, these corpulent Greek women are as excessively extended, as bodily over-twisted and spatially curved as purely Cubist creations. These compositions of stout corporeal shapes are the prelude to a new balancing, a re-examination, a diagnosis, not in the quantitative, but in the qualitative sense. These objects and their limbs are being examined on their real value, the value of their action power within a larger relationship. Fingers are turned into brushes

13

because they are not fit for anything else, or into knives and scissors if the reference is to their being employed for cutting and dividing up, or again into rags because they serve no other purpose (Plate 19). An arm is visibly propped up, thus revealing its function as a prop and its relationship to a pillar. A body is pressed into a chair whose legs, therefore, must be more firmly straddled. Boots stamp the ground and turn into hooves. There is a bulge where the neck of the woman merges into her bust, so that the blouse may be held in place. One mouth is turned into a gaping gullet, another into a mincing-machine. A face, seen in profile, resembles a beak, and at the same time, seen *en face*, a goggle-eyed pair of glasses. An inward-sucking gaze becomes a pair of eyes which grip like pincers. Léger effects such transformations symbolically, as though in a vacuum (plate 23). Picasso, on the other hand, actually succeeds in dislodging reality with the help of these exaggerations. It was a condition of this functional style that the voluminous should be accentuated, that just as during the analytical phase the unity of time and space had been destroyed, so in the synthetic phase form must be untwined, and the object interlocked with form.

One might assume that henceforth recollection was replaced by observation. But this is true only insofar as Picasso was no longer concerned with retained impressions of the objective world, but resolved to plumb far deeper, into the realm of arch-images. After these had been subjected to the X-ray analysis of reality, they functioned as transmittors into metaphysics.

Much has been said here about the theory underlying Cubist art, and most people may feel that their experience of art has little to do with theory. But we should not forget that for more than four centuries we have applied, without being aware of it, the conception of painting which came in with the Renaissance. We must now remember to discard it whenever we look at pictures. We must realize that a theory which has rapidly lost ground since Cézanne can only prevent us from understanding a new way of painting as revolutionary in its way as painting was around 1400. There may be some use, after all, in grappling with a few theoretical arguments if thereby we learn to decipher modern art. Spontaneous experience anyhow comes either naturally or not at all. Those who detest theory, however, should have put this book aside after the first few pages — it's too late for that now!

LIST OF ILLUSTRATIONS

Plate 1

Georges Braque (born 1882 at Argenteuil)

LANDSCAPE OF ESTAQUE

Oil, painted 1908

Musée National d'Art Moderne, Paris

A painting belonging to the early phase of Cubism. The landscape is interpreted as a world precipitating itself head over heels. Trees, mountains, and the sky surge up like an enormous breaker. The path retreats zig-zag fashion into the background, flanked by bulging, ball-shaped trees. The sky reaches across the whole *is* with giant sickles. One has the impression that the picture is rotating around the jerking axle of the road, its upper part moving towards the right, its lower part towards the left. The painting is far removed from the Latin mellowness of Cézanne, who died two years before it was made. The vehemence of the brush stroke and the attempt at a tremendous movement in space unexpectedly cut short, rather resemble German Expressionism, which arrived at similar seismic visions.

Plate 2

Fernand Léger (born 1881 at Argentan, died 1955)

VILLAGE LANDSCAPE

Oil, painted around 1911

Kunsthistorisches Museum, Vienna

There is less turbulence in Léger's paintings than in those by Picasso and Braque of a few years earlier. This canvas is the Cubist impression of a real landscape, and it is a fresh and graceful impression, clear and bright as glass. It is somewhat further removed from reality than a truly Impressionist landscape, but retains much that is traditional, and is therefore helpful in training the eye to assimilate the Cubist method. Trees resemble soap bubbles or blown-up balloons, they are light and transparent. The whole picture is filled and compact like a glass cube. The trees on the right look like gramophone records, the trunks like surveyors' rods (red at the bottom, white in the middle, blue at the top). It all strikes one as rather artificial, strongly resembling a stage set. Sets, in a similar way, give but a limited illusion of depth. To achieve this, however, is not one of the aims of Léger, and even in this picture light does cast shadows. The painting is framed, on the left by the corner of a house, on the right by the trees shaped like gramophone records; at the bottom, left and right, circular accents balance each other. Yet the traditional vista is barred and devalued, as for instance on the far right where the red triangular roof seemingly lies further in the foreground than the tree. The white holes in the picture, too, block the prospect. Disarrangements such as this derive from Cézanne who in his pictures balanced area against space. Thus a kind of dynamic box-room is created, and Cézanne's prescription ("Everything in nature is shaped like a globe, a cube and a cylinder") is put to the test by Léger.

Plate 3

Pablo Picasso (born 1881 at Malaga)

WOMAN WITH MANDOLIN

Oil

Penrose Collection, London

Looking at this painting, one is all too ready to recall the slogan of the "destruction of form". But in fact this is confusing the issues. Not the form, but the subject has apparently been destroyed: in this case the woman with the mandolin who is part of a palpable and therefore destructible world. Far from being wrecked, form is used in a rhythmical manner to build up this picture; it cannot possibly therefore be a portrayal of palpable reality, but must be considered as an independent creation. Nor, incidentally, should the sharp-edged, fragmentary quality of the painting be mistaken for a symptom of "destruction". A certain resemblance to reality which is retained only enhances its decidedly uninviting, remote, unapproachable, and rather forbidding self-sufficiency. Can it be that Picasso was thinking of Jean Fouquet's "Madonna of Melun"?

It will be seen that the sculptural cohesion, the sculptural rhythm of the various components is broken up, and that sharp-edged, solitary parts are set against each other and accentuated. This is done in order to thicken space in this painting, by filling it to bursting-point. Still, even here there is no notion yet of non-Euclidian space. Were Leonardo da Vinci alive today, were he to have helped to shape, along with Einstein and Planck, a new conception of the universe on the lines of modern physics, perhaps, after inventing the jet plane and after planning a journey to the moon on a thermo-nuclear basis, he would paint his "Madonna of the Rocks" along similar lines.

Plate 15

Juan Gris (born 1887, died 1927)

THE PIERROT

Oil, painted 1919

Musée National d'Art Moderne, Paris

There are machines of which the parts join without gaps in faultless precision (cogwheels, a work-bench, etc.). So, here, the positive and the negative, degrees of light and shade are joined. The figure penetrates the wall as a key enters its lock. The key is first put into the lock, then turned in a different direction; it is therefore used first *en face*, then in profile.

This figure is simultaneously filtered through the area, incorporated into the area, in two dimensions. It is by no means simply a stereometric reproduction.

A figure like a secret door in a tapestry. A mute phenomenon. A symbol in Braille.

Plate 16

Pablo Picasso (born 1881)

STILL-LIFE WITH ANTIQUE HEAD

Oil, painted 1925

Musée National d'Art Moderne, Paris

Here light and shade are not attached to outlines or bodies, but move freely. Light creates negative space, brightness is colour scratched out. Light and shade no longer mean bright and dark. Light by-passes several objects, then fills another entirely, creeps on like a puddle, overflows. Light and shade obstinately insist on their separate existence beside objects which, in the hierarchy of the picture, belong to a caste threatened by death. Thus, exposed to peril, they appear to be more individual by a few degrees than in real life. The weapon of light is razor-sharpness, the weapon of shade is dull force. Individual features of things are reduced to a faint glimmer. The bowl turned into a moon idol is a symbol of the new reign.

Plate 17

Georges Braque (born 1882)

STILL-LIFE WITH MARBLE TABLE

Oil, painted 1925

Musée National d'Art Moderne, Paris

There is always, in these Cubist still-life paintings, one dominant impression like a key in music.

In the preceding picture it was the vibrating discussion between light and the colour of coffee brown, here it is the streaky, flickering effect. The whole painting resembles a polished marble slab and the still-life in its middle some fossilization which has emerged under polishing — petrified shell or primeval fish. The fossilized primeval ocean is seen as wall panelling and offsets a cornucopia of fruit — *frutta di mare*. This picture has its settled focus in the piled-up buffet on the right to which lead, in geological formations, the shifting plates on the left. There is a direct link between a "bourgeois" still-life of Braque's such as this and the 19th century French painters.

Plate 18

Fernand Léger (born 1881, died 1955)

COMPOSITION WITH THREE FIGURES

Oil, painted 1932

Musée National d'Art Moderne, Paris

This picture exemplifies the predominance of the sculptural over the linear form in Cubist painting. At this period of his work Léger increasingly characterizes objects by heavy contours and strong lines; they are held as though by the ropes of a farm cart, and the sausage-like shape of the figures expresses their idle, stolid and plebeian cast. Joints are shown in pictorial rather than anatomical terms, especially in later paintings. Figures become detached from their background and acquire the solid corporeality of sculpture. To Léger, as to Picasso and Braque, the problem was this: how to make these sculptural figures cohere with the background without destroying the surface of the picture. It now began to appear that in painting background is the medium of time. When there is no background the picture becomes immobile, statuesque, and disconnected. The figures or objects exist in space but not time, and Cubism in this form draws near sculpture. In his later years Léger concentrated almost entirely on frescoes, the masterpiece among which is "The Great Parade" — a circus scene, painted shortly before his death.

Plate 19

Pablo Picasso (born 1881)

PORTRAIT OF A WOMAN

Oil, painted 1948

Musée National d'Art Moderne, Paris

This portrait is painted with muscular vehemence, notably the horizontal stripes of the woman's jumper. The paint used was fairly liquid and allowed to run, to spill over edges drawn by brush-strokes. But despite its apparent freedom the painting is "organized". There is not an arbitrary line in it. On the posts of the chair the colour applied is somewhat drier, while on the face it is scraped. There are hardly any areas of colour on this canvas; its structure consists entirely of outlines or striped fillings. It might be called a "graphic" picture, but the term is inadequate. These lines are charged with energy, and the "iron towers" of the chair posts might form part of a suspension bridge or a radio tower. All this recurs in the woman's energetic and severe profile.

How is she presented? The skirt is taut, the bust soft in profile and rounded *en face*. The arm smoothly laid over the arm-rest is thickset. The right hand is spread out, the left unfolds like a crown of leaves. Chair posts and arm rests jut out in various directions. The neck resembles the stem of a goblet, and sits on a firm horizontal stroke. The profile of the head is drawn with a swing, deriving its force from the jaw-line. Front view and side view are fused into one. The hair is used as a frame, shadow and background.

In this way the painter shows a number of movements, of motions joined to each other like transmission wheels. It is not action itself which is represented (for action here is different — calm and immobile) but action transmitted and transferred, the effect of leverage. A chair normally just *is*, but here its posts jut out and seem electrically charged. One's eye penetrates the picture in various directions — into the organism of the sitting figure, remarkably erect without the use of shoulders, for which the thrusting chair is a substitute. This picture might have been painted by a still wilder, yet more acute Van Gogh.

Plate 20

Pablo Picasso (born 1881)

THE SERENADE

Oil, painted 1942

Musée National d'Art Moderne, Paris

The world represented here differs fundamentally from that commonly shown in painting, or for that matter, from the associations evoked by a serenade. It appears to be seen through a particular kind of coloured pair of spectacles; the construction is entirely of prisms. In this world everything is pointed and interlocking in angles; even space becomes a corner alcove.

Picasso has given the impression in this picture of a world cut up by a knife; instead of the soothing melody of the traditional serenade this music seems to inflict pain. Even the couch appears at first glance to be a rack, a Procrustean bed of torture.

Plate 21

Pablo Picasso (born 1881)

FEMALE HEAD

Oil, painted October 15th, 1939

Collection Martha Widmer, Winterthur

First opinion: This is a hideous picture, a distortion of the human face, a mockery of man. To the conventional Christian and Humanist beholder this sort of painting seems like a perversion of "the beautiful", and to evoke primitive cults of black magic.

Second opinion: This figure, like a hedgehog or a fungoid volcano bursting from the crater of a collar, with its wounded eye and clashing lines, mirrors the catastrophic predicament of modern man. The picture was painted just after the outbreak of war, and may perhaps be indicative of the existentialist point of view.

Third opinion: This is a colourful and gay painting, sparkling like fireworks. The features move briskly like the sails of a windmill, and the head suggests a paper kite poking its nose into the open air. This one may call the aesthetic point of view, from which paintings like this are remarkable for their pictorial design.

It is admissible today to hold any of these three opinions. No one philosophy of life satisfies everyone, and with the many conflicting systems of thought go many conflicting emotional reactions to art. Good evidence of the emergence of new ways of thought may be seen in the widely varying but equally strong artistic personalities.

Plate 22

Georges Braque (born 1882)

THE BILLIARD TABLE

Oil, painted 1945

Musée National d'Art Moderne, Paris

Many of Braque's pictures have some connection with the sea, with under-water life, with aquariums. The billiard table is not broken in half, as one might think, but the crack which runs through the whole picture is merely the symbol for "broken", "reflected". The metamorphic character which is so strongly pronounced in the Cubist paintings of Picasso also plays an important part with Braque, although here it is not expressed directly, but reflected in his objects, which suffer a sea-change.

The transformation suffered in this painting by a middle-class drawing-room seems to turn all objects into a minor "landscape in eclipse". The green mirror of the billiard table is the surface of a puddle opening into the deep, and traversed by reeds. The billiard-cue becomes a reed-mace. Everything is in autumn tints. The room recalls a log-cabin, and the billiard table is like a rowing-boat, sinking. The billiard balls seem like water-lilies, the red one a flower growing in a swamp.

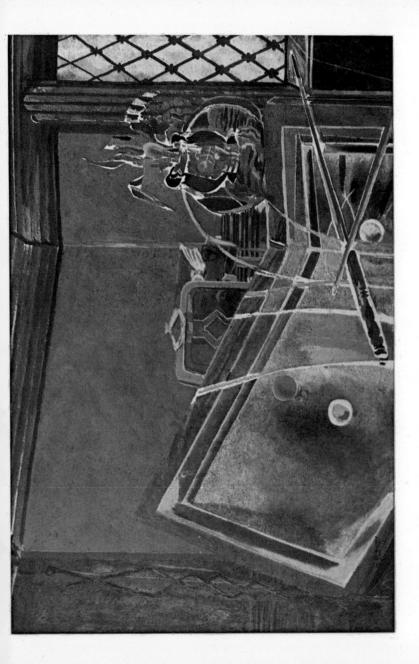

Plate 23

Fernand Léger (born 1881, died 1955)

ADIEU, NEW YORK

Oil, painted 1946

Musée National d'Art Moderne, Paris

A good example of Léger's mature style.

His paintings are often frescoes compressed into easel-paintings. In his later pictures Léger is fond of inserting stripes of colour; these are garish, gay, and unrelated to objects, for they run over the outlines. These unbroken patches of colour are mainly primary colours — red, blue, green, yellow — not mixed but transferred to the canvas as though squeezed from a tube or put on as a decorator might paint. The initial elements of imitative painting remain in the shadows and raised surfaces, but the colour as a whole has no realistic meaning.

Not only the colours but also the actual objects painted have this quality of solidity and isolation; the wheel, the sun shaped like a coxcomb, are in pieces, but the pieces themselves are intact and realistic. Objects fly through the air or are shaken like handkerchiefs in farewell; everything seems to wave, and the whole effect is somewhat like a Red Indian dance performed in farewell at the airport.

Plate 24

Rufino Tamayo (born 1899 at Oaxaca, Mexico)

THE SINGER

Oil, painted 1950

Musée National d'Art Moderne, Paris

Tamayo's parents were Zapotec Indians. Originally he was interested in music. In 1917 he began to paint, and in 1923 became professor at the Academy of Arts in Mexico City. In 1938 he settled in New York, but since 1953 has returned to Mexico. Today he is considered one of his country's most important painters. In his art Cubism is allied to popular Mexican elements.